MILESTONES

IN THE EVOLUTION OF GOVERNMENT

LEEANNE GELLETLY

MC

MASON CREST
PHILADELPHIA

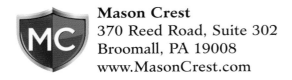

Mason Crest
370 Reed Road, Suite 302
Broomall, PA 19008
www.MasonCrest.com

Printed and bound in the United States of America

CPSIA Compliance Information: Batch #MEG2012-5. For further information, contact Mason Crest at 1-866-MCP-Book.

First printing
1 3 5 7 9 8 6 4 2

Library of Congress Cataloging-in-Publication Data

Gelletly, LeeAnne.
Milestones in the evolution of government / LeeAnne Gelletly.
    p. cm. — (Major forms of world government)
Includes bibliographical references and index.
ISBN 978-1-4222-2140-2 (hc)
ISBN 978-1-4222-9457-4 (ebook)
1. Comparative government. 2. State, The. I. Title.
JF51.G45 2013
321.009—dc23
                        2012027845

Publisher's note: All quotations in this book are taken from original sources, and contain the spelling and grammatical inconsistencies of the original texts.

TITLES IN THIS SERIES

COMMUNISM

DEMOCRACY

DICTATORSHIP

FASCISM

MILESTONES

IN THE EVOLUTION

OF GOVERNMENT

MONARCHY

OLIGARCHY

THEOCRACY

TABLE OF CONTENTS

    by Dr. Timothy Colton, Chairman
    Department of Government, Harvard University

INTRODUCTION by Dr. Timothy Colton, Harvard University

When human beings try to understand complex sets of things, they usually begin by sorting them into categories. They classify or group the phenomena that interest them into boxes that are basically very much alike. These boxes can then be compared and analyzed. The logic of classification applies to the study of inanimate objects (such as, for example, bodies of water or minerals), to living organisms (such as species of birds or bacteria), and also to man-made systems (such as religions or communications media).

This series of short books is about systems of government, which are specific and very important kinds of man-made systems. Systems of government are arrangements for human control and cooperation on particular territories. Governments dispense justice, make laws, raise taxes, fight wars, run school and health systems, and perform many other services that we often take for granted. Like, say, minerals, bacteria, and religions, systems of government come in a wide variety of forms or categories.

Just what are those categories? One of the earliest attempts to answer this question rigorously was made in the fourth century BCE by the brilliant Greek philosopher Aristotle. His study *Politics* has come down to us in incomplete form, as many of his writings were lost after he died. Nonetheless, it contains a simple and powerful scheme for classifying systems of government. Aristotle researched and illustrated his treatise by looking at the constitutions of 158 small city-states near the eastern shores of the Mediterranean Sea of his day, most of them inhabited by Greeks.

According to Aristotle's *Politics*, any system of government could be accurately classified and thus understood once two things were known. The first was, how many people were involved in making political decisions: one person, a small number, or a large number. The second issue was whether the system was designed to serve the common good of the citizens of the city-state. Taken together, these distinctions produced six categories of governmental system in all: monarchy (rule by one civic-minded person); tyranny (rule by one selfish person); aristocracy (rule by the few in the interests of all); oligarchy (rule by the few to suit themselves); constitutional government or "polity" (rule by the many in the common interest); and finally a form of mob rule (rule by the many with no concern for the greater good).

The fifth of these classic categories comes closest to modern representative democracy, as it is experienced in the United States, Western Europe, India, and many other places. One of the things Aristotle teaches us, however, is that there are many alternatives to this setup. In addition to the volume on democracy, this Mason Crest series will acquaint students with systems of government that correspond in rough terms to other categories invented by Aristotle more than two thousand years ago. These include monarchy; dictatorship (in Aristotle's terms, tyranny); oligarchy; communism (which we might think of as a particular kind of modern-day oligarchy); fascism (which combines some of the characteristics of tyranny and mob rule); and theocracy (which does not fit easily into Aristotle's scheme, although we might think of it as tyranny or oligarchy, but in the name of some divine being or creed).

Aristotle focused his research on the written constitutions of city-states. Today, political scientists, with better tools at their disposal, delve more into the actual practice of government in different countries. That practice frequently differs from the theory written into the constitution. Scholars study why it is that countries differ so much in terms of how and in whose interests governmental decisions are taken, across broad categories and within these categories, as well as in mixed systems that cross the boundaries between categories. It turns out that there are not one but many reasons for these differences, and there are significant disagreements about which reasons are most important. Some of the reasons are examined in this book series.

Experts on government also wonder a lot about trends over time. Why is it that some version of democracy has come to be the most common form of government in the contemporary world? Why has democratization come in distinct waves, with long periods of stagnation or even of reverse de-democratization separating them? The so-called third wave of democratization began in the 1970s and extended into the 1990s, and featured, among other changes, the collapse of communist systems in the Soviet Union and Eastern Europe and the disintegration of differently constituted nondemocratic systems in Southern Europe and Latin America. At the present time, the outlook for democracy is uncertain. In a number of Arab countries, authoritarian systems of government have recently been overthrown or challenged by revolts. And yet, it is far from clear that the result will be functioning democracies. Moreover, it is far from clear that the world will not encounter another wave of de-democratization. Nor can we rule out the rise of fundamentally new forms of government not foreseen by Aristotle; these might be encouraged by contemporary forms of technology and communication, such as the Internet, behavioral tracking devices, and social media.

For young readers to be equipped to consider complex questions like these, they need to begin with the basics about existing and historical systems of government. It is to meet their educational needs that this book series is aimed.

East German police and West German citizens watch as a workman dismantles a section of the Berlin Wall at Potsdamer Platz, November 1989. For nearly 30 years, the wall symbolized the division of Germany into two states with very different systems of government.

1

FROM SUBJECT TO CITIZEN

On November 9, 1989, tens of thousands of cheering people celebrated the fall of a concrete wall in Berlin. Some of them took hammers and chisels to the hated symbol, intent on breaking it apart. They were East Germans, exulting in their new freedom to travel across the border from the east to the west. Since 1961, that had not been possible. For 28 years the Berlin Wall had stopped them.

A POLITICAL MILESTONE

The wall was built by a repressive government called the German Democratic Republic. The nation's name did not reflect the true ideology of the GDR, which was neither democratic nor a republic. In a democracy, all people have the right to participate in government. In a republic, citizens vote for the government officials who represent them. The GDR was a repressive state run by a single political party—the Socialist Unity Party of Germany, also known as the East German Communist Party.

The East German government allowed its people few freedoms. It controlled all economic aspects of the country. And it used the press "to direct the thinking of the people into correct political lines." In August 1961, to stop the thousands of people from fleeing East Germany each day, the GDR—with massive support from the Soviet Union—had closed its border to the west. Ultimately a 12-foot-tall, 27-mile-long concrete wall, topped by barbed wire, divided the city of Berlin. East German guards manned the watchtowers. They were under orders to shoot to kill anyone attempting to cross into West Berlin. Over the years almost two hundred people died in the attempt.

Autocratic communist regimes had held power for decades in Eastern Europe and the Soviet Union. But in the late 1980s many of them were self-destructing. The fall of the Berlin Wall in 1989 symbolized the collapse of communism and the rise of new freedoms. Many former communist countries would transition to democratic governments in which citizens could vote in free, multiparty elections. When the Berlin Wall fell, people across Eastern Europe celebrated a major milestone. Authoritarian communist governments were making way for governments that would protect human rights and dignity.

> German sociologist Max Weber (1864–1920) described a state as a government that has the right to use force to maintain control. "[A] state is a human community," he wrote, "that (successfully) claims the monopoly of the legitimate use of physical force within a given territory."

KINDS OF GOVERNMENT

A government is the body or system by which a state, community, or people are controlled or regulated. The word govern comes from the Latin word *gubernare*, which means "to steer" or "to rule." In an organized society, government is the authority or body that controls, influences, or regulates the policies, actions, and affairs of a state. Among a state's primary goals are achieving order and providing security.

Civilization has seen the rise and fall of hundreds of thousands of governments. In ancient times monarchy, or rule by one person, was common. Some monarchal governments were long-lasting regimes in which the son or daughter inherited the throne upon the monarch's death. Such hereditary monarchies existed in ancient times in many parts of the world, including Africa (Egypt), the Middle East (Mesopotamia), India, and China.

In some cases, the central authority was not a king but an individual who seized power and ruled by force. In early times, this government was called a tyranny. It is referred to today as a dictatorship. In other cases a small elite group held power. This form of government was an oligarchy.

Throughout world history, there have been many different types of governments. In Central America, the ancient Maya established city-states under the control of ruling families. This stone sculpture, representing a Mayan king, was taken from his tomb at the Palenque site in Mexico's Yucatán Peninsula.

In monarchies and tyrannies, a single person controlled the state. In oligarchies, a small elite group was in charge. But in some ancient Greek city-states, democracy became the form of government. In these democratic governments citizens exercised power as voters, jurists, and members of assemblies. They did not submit to a supreme authority.

But the power of the citizen lasted only about two hundred years. It was lost in the centuries that followed in governments where the individual was expected to be obedient to the state. But even as the state maintained authority, new forms of government continued to develop. One of them was the republic, which first appeared in ancient Rome around 500 BC. A republic was a representative form of government. Roman citizens elected public officials to represent them.

Laws and rules made by ancient kings gave way to rules established by lawmaking bodies of men. Known as senates, parliaments, and assemblies,

President Barack Obama speaks to members of the U.S. Congress. The United States is a federal republic, in which governing authority is divided between the national government and state and local governments.

these groups helped establish the rule of law within their societies. The rule of law refers to well-defined and established public rules and written law. In modern times it is usually part of a written constitution—the document that creates a government and defines and limits its functions.

> Laws are the systems of rules regulating the actions of members of society.

MODERN GOVERNMENTS

Political scientist Francis Fukuyama has written that there are three political institutions essential to political order: the state (a centralized authority), the rule of law, and accountability (the idea of being subordinate to the will of the people). The first two institutions, he explains, developed in early civilizations. The third did not appear until modern times, when the individual rights of people gained importance.

As citizens' rights were recognized, the rule of law limited the power of rulers. A constitution, for example, establishes a government of laws in which the rule of law applies to all, including the ruler. Constitutions can require a ruler to be accountable to parliaments, assemblies, or other groups representing the people.

Accountability, thus, is an idea that is an element of the modern state. It reflects the idea that people are the supreme authority in government. Accordingly it is used most often in describing democratic governments. With democracy came the new ideas of the state's responsibility to its people, including protecting the rights of citizens. Fukuyama identifies liberal democracies as the most widely endorsed form of a just government.

LIBERAL DEMOCRACY

In a liberal democracy, citizens decide who will govern them. They have the right to participate in free and fair elections to select their government. There are no gender, racial, or ethnic limits in defining citizenship. In elections, the government allows universal suffrage—all adult citizens have the right to vote.

KEY IDEA

Three major elements of a modern state are a system of centralized authority, the rule of law, and accountability.

Citizens of a liberal democracy can also have faith that the government will protect their fundamental rights. Such rights include the right to free speech, the right to choose one's religion, and the right to fair legal proceedings if accused of a crime. Property rights are protected and people have the right to consent to policies that affect them.

At the turn of the 20th century, most of the world's governments were monarchies. In 2012, according to the Washington, D.C.–based Freedom House, fully 60 percent of countries (117 out of 195) were electoral democracies. This means citizens have the right to vote for their government in elections. (Freedom House is a U.S. government–funded organization that evaluates governments' defense of political rights and civil liberties in countries around the world.)

CITIZENS' RIGHTS

Over the course of human history government has evolved from authoritarianism to accountability and protection of citizens' rights. Along the way, the concept of citizenship also evolved, with full political rights being extended to an ever-wider portion of the population. Initially, the United States, France, Great Britain, and other early democracies of the modern era allowed only a small minority of their people—free men who owned significant amounts of property—to vote or hold office. Gradually property requirements were eased, giving more and more men the right to vote. Women won the franchise only later. Such changes would be milestones in the development of the state.

The evolution of government through history reflected changes in thinking about human rights and equality. When the rights of the individual were asserted in government, the subject gained rights that made him—and her—a citizen.

2

THE STATE AND THE LAW

In prehistoric times people formed tight-knit groups. These small bands consisted of extended family members. And in these bands the individual's primary loyalty was to his or her kinfolk.

TRIBES AND CHIEFDOMS

Eventually bands merged to form larger groups, or tribes. Most members of tribes identified themselves as having a common ancestry, which meant there were still blood ties. People were nomadic, traveling from place to place in search of food for themselves or their livestock. As the need arose, tribes moved their tents and possessions to other lands.

The tribe was typically led by a chief or "big man." The chief was usually bigger, stronger, or smarter than his subjects. He often came to power because he was better at hunting or in battle.

Among the nomadic tribes of the ancient world, those who possessed the largest flocks were considered to be wealthy and blessed by the gods. They were the most likely to become leaders of their tribe.

Chiefs were the head of their people. But because tribes were nomadic, their leaders did not assert control over land.

THE FIRST STATES

It was not until the invention of agriculture around 8000 BC that many tribal groups established permanent settlements. Early villages headed by a tribal chief sprang up on fertile lands near rivers. In agricultural societies control over the land was important. And this control of territory by a centralized source of authority—the chief—represented the establishment of the first states.

The chief handled decisions affecting the settlement, such as when or where to hunt or fish, plant crops, or pasture livestock. Some chiefs entered into trade agreements with other villages. Or they formed alliances with them to protect their village from attacks or to battle other groups. Conflict was common as villages sought to control territorial boundaries and access to water.

Alliances between villages led to the formation of chiefdoms in which a centralized authority, or paramount chief, held authority over numerous villages and communities. His sons commonly succeeded him upon his death. The result was the development of an elite class descended from the ruling family.

With the development of agriculture, humans began to settle into communities such as Harappa, an ancient city in the Indus Valley, in modern-day Pakistan. The picture shows the excavated remains of a large well (upper left) and a stone platform (lower right). Harappa was inhabited more than 4,500 years ago and is believed to have supported a population in excess of 20,000, making it one of the largest cities of the Bronze Age.

SOCIAL HIERARCHY

As chiefdoms grew, some of them made agricultural advancements, such as the development of extensive irrigation systems, which greatly increased the food supply. In various regions the population exploded, and villages evolved into substantial cities or city-states. By around 4000 BC there were urban areas supporting thousands of people in the Middle East along the Euphrates and Tigris Rivers (Mesopotamia) and in northeast Africa along the Nile River (Egypt). Large states also emerged in the Indus Valley of India, and along the Yellow River in China.

Within these large cities, society grew more complex. A hierarchy of social classes developed in which people held specific jobs. At the top were monarchs and elite rulers. At the bottom were farmers and slaves. In between were priests, soldiers, administrators, and craftsmen. The lower classes—the craftsmen and farmers—supported the ruling classes by paying taxes and tribute to the king. In exchange, the king and a growing elite ruling class established law and order. The monarch also maintained peace by controlling warriors needed to defend the community against neighboring tribes and states.

As larger civilizations developed, rulers created armies to wage war against enemies and maintain order in their domains. This relief sculpture from an ancient Mesopotamian palace depicts a group of Assyrian soldiers.

"WAR MADE THE STATE"

Armies and soldiers were essential to the formation of large states. With claims to land came conflict as varying groups asserted ownership of territory. Kings led armies to acquire land or protect their regimes from other forces. One of the first large civilizations, Sumer, in Mesopotamia, was founded around 3500 BC. It had a police force and an army headed by the king.

Historian Charles Tilly has described the process in which modern states emerged with the simple phrase: "War made the state and the state made war." The idea of such ongoing warfare can be applied to early empires as well. By acquiring land, states became more powerful. As states conquered other lands, they commonly imposed their laws and cultures on the defeated peoples, and they established bureaucracies to administer conquered territories.

The result was the formation of empires—a group of states ruled by a supreme authority. In western Asia, major empires led by monarchies included the Akkadian, Babylonian, Assyrian, Persian, and Roman Empires. The latter two would develop impressive roads and administration systems that enabled the centralized government to maintain control over its conquered territories.

> "LIFE, LIBERTY AND PROPERTY DO NOT EXIST BECAUSE MEN HAVE MADE LAWS. ON THE CONTRARY, IT WAS THE FACT THAT LIFE, LIBERTY, AND PROPERTY EXISTED BEFOREHAND THAT CAUSED MEN TO MAKE LAWS IN THE FIRST PLACE."
>
> —FRENCH ECONOMIST FRÉDÉRIC BASTIAT (1801–1850)

RULE OF LAW

The development of writing helped government officials, or bureaucrats, administer large governments. And it also allowed monarchs to make their rules and laws known to the public.

Ancient kings were absolute rulers. Their word was law. By putting that word in writing, the rules of their society were established as the rule of law.

The Chinese philosopher Confucius taught that rulers had a responsibility to act in the best interests of their people, while the people had a responsibility to support and obey the ruler. Confucian teachings became an underlying principle of government during the Han dynasty, which ruled China from 206 BC until AD 220. Most subsequent Chinese ruling dynasties would continue to rely heavily on the teachings of Confucius, until the end of China's dynastic system in the early 20th century.

Some historians believe that around 3300 BC the king of Egypt—the pharaoh Menes—first put laws into writing. The first written legal code (a complete system of laws) that exists today came from the Mesopotamian king Ur-Nammu of the Sumerian civilization. It was produced around 2100–2050 BC.

Between about 1780 and 1750 BC the founder of the Babylonian Empire, King Hammurabi, established and publicized a code of laws. These Babylonian laws, known today as the Code of Hammurabi, were inscribed on large stone pillars, or stelae, for display in cities of the realm. Among the concepts included was the presumption of innocence and the idea that both the accused and accuser should have the opportunity to provide evidence.

In ancient China, the teachings of the philosopher Confucius (ca. 551–478 BC) also contributed to law. Confucius stressed that governments were united and stabilized through "cultivation of virtue." A few hundred years after his death the Chinese government would adopt his ethical teachings as a basis for government.

DIVINE RULE

In monarchies, subjects felt loyal to the state when they believed in the ruler's authority to rule. For centuries, that authority was linked to religious authority. Some early monarchs, such as the Egyptian pharaohs, claimed to be gods. Others served as spiritual leaders whose role was to bring order and prosperity to their people by performing ceremonies and leading sacrificial rites. They were believed to use their divine powers to assure rich harvests and protection from disasters such as floods or plagues. As god-kings, they could wield absolute power, for they were not to be questioned.

ATHENIAN DEMOCRACY

In opposition to the idea of absolute monarchy was the emergence of democracy, a system of government in which power rests with ordinary citizens. The word *democracy* comes from the Greek word *demos*, meaning "the people," and *kratos*, meaning "power" or "rule."

Democracy was introduced in the Greek city-state of Athens around 500 BC. It flourished in the century that followed, spreading to other Greek city-states.

Athens had a direct democracy. Athenians didn't elect lawmakers to represent them. Instead, all adult male citizens had the right to vote directly on proposed legislation in an assembly. If a measure received a majority of votes, it passed. A smaller council that set the agenda for the assembly was staffed with citizens chosen at random for one-year terms. The same method was used to fill most administrative positions and to select juries for trials.

The idea of kings holding divine status existed all over the world. Egyptian pharaohs and the Inca emperors of South America were considered gods. The Chinese emperor was said to rule by the "mandate of heaven." And the Japanese emperor was believed to be a descendant of the goddess of the sun.

In Athens, which had a direct democracy from about 500 to 338 BC, the assembly of citizens met at this hill, called the Pnyx. About 6,000 people could fit on the hill to discuss and vote on issues related to the city's governance. The carved steps in the center lead to the speaker's platform.

During the mid-fifth century BC, Athens entered a golden age of democracy after the statesman Pericles helped pass reforms, such as the payment of salaries for government service, that allowed poor people to participate fully in the political process.

Still, only a minority of the people living in Athens had any voice in the government. To begin, all women were excluded from the Athenian democracy. So, too, were slaves, who made up at least a quarter of the population but couldn't be citizens. People who were born outside of Athens, and people with a parent who wasn't an Athenian citizen, could never become citizens either. So for all its achievements, democracy in Athens—and democracy across ancient Greece—was quite limited.

In 338 BC Philip of Macedon conquered Greece. This effectively put an end to democracy in the Greek city-states.

THE REPUBLIC OF ANCIENT ROME

With the rise of Rome, new political institutions emerged. According to tradition, the city of Rome was founded in 753 BC and ruled for more than two centuries by elected kings. The kings were advised by a group of elders who formed an assembly called the Senate. Around 509 BC, the monarchy was overthrown and Rome became a republic.

A republic was a new form of government. The word *republic* comes from the Latin *res publica*, which means "public property" or "public affairs." This referred to the idea that citizens exercised political power. In

Rome's republican government, citizens elected public officials to represent them and run the state. But as in Athens, women in Rome couldn't vote, and slaves weren't citizens and had no rights at all. In addition, the Roman system concentrated political power in the hands of the landowning upper class, called the patricians. Only patricians could serve in the Senate, and they held most other high offices as well. However, the lower class, or plebeians (which included craftspeople, merchants, and small farmers), did elect lower-ranking officials.

> Some political philosophers theorize that the loss of human freedoms occurred first with the emergence of monarchy. When people gave obedience to the king, they relinquished their "equal rights" to participate in government.

BRANCHES OF GOVERNMENT

The constitution of the Roman Republic was not written down, or codified. What is known about how it worked comes from Marcus Tullius Cicero, a statesman who lived during the time of the Republic. Cicero described a mixed constitution, with elements of three forms of government: monarchy, aristocracy, and democracy.

The Roman Republic's monarchical element lay with high officials. At the top were two magistrates, called consuls. These civil and military leaders were elected to one-year terms. They held *imperium*—supreme executive and judicial authority, including the power to command armies. Other high officials in the Republic included *praetors*, who served as governors; and *quaestors*, who administered the state treasury.

In Cicero's view, the Senate represented aristocracy in Rome's republican government. It was an unelected council composed entirely of patricians. Senators were typically former magistrates. Although the Senate didn't have the authority to make laws, it enacted decrees guiding state policy, advised magistrates, and controlled finances (except during wartime).

The writings of Cicero helped scholars understand the government of the Roman Republic.

The democratic element in the Republic consisted of various people's assemblies. In these assemblies citizens voted for officials and passed laws. One type of assembly (*comitia*) was open to all citizens. Another type (*concilium*) was composed of a specific category of people—for example, soldiers or plebeians. Tribunes elected by the plebeian assembly were particularly important in protecting the interests of the lower class.

ROMAN IDEAS

Concerns that individuals or groups might gain too much power resulted in a system of government based on checks and balances. For example, the tribunes had the power to veto elections or decrees of the Senate. The Senate had the authority to interpret laws passed by assemblies.

Founders of future governments would emulate the concept of checks and balances. They would also adopt other ideas that originated with the Roman Republic. These included the veto, impeachment, and regularly scheduled elections. And one of the most important political institutions—the republic itself—would serve as a basis for the development of later forms of government.

ROMAN LAW

The Roman Republic lasted about 500 years. Around the first century

BC, the emperor Caesar Augustus took command of the government and created the Roman Empire. The empire would span a vast territory along the Mediterranean Sea and dominate the region for several centuries. During that time the Romans created a highly developed system of laws. Some were social rules—customs and traditions that were formalized as written laws. Other laws were formal rules used to organize the way power was distributed in the system. And still others dealt with the concept of property rights. Rights to property were enforced by courts and legal systems that had the power to settle disputes.

Around AD 400, the empire split into eastern and western halves. The Eastern Roman Empire—which included today's Turkey, Greece, the Balkans, and the Middle East—would become known as the Byzantine Empire after the fall of the Western Roman Empire in the late fifth century. In 534, under the Byzantine emperor Justinian, Roman law was codified. It became the basis for later legal systems, particularly those of governments in continental Europe.

Roman Catholic leaders (left) and military supporters (right) attend the coronation of a German king in this illustration from the Middle Ages.

3

AUTHORITY AND LEGITIMACY

Hereditary monarchy remained the dominant form of government during the Middle Ages in Europe (from around 500 to around 1500). Kings and queens held great secular power. But political power also lay in the hands of the Roman Catholic Church. According to the Church, religious law superseded secular law. And the authority of the Church in legitimizing the rule of a monarch greatly influenced people's acceptance of that ruler.

European monarchs claimed that their authority to rule came from God and expressed God's will. Roman Catholic Church leaders reinforced this claim by participating in coronation ceremonies (the official crowning of a monarch). The coronation ritual involved the pope or another religious leader anointing the king or queen with holy chrism, a mixture of oil and aromatic resins. The religious ritual of anointment affirmed the divine right of the king or queen to rule.

FEUDAL SOCIETY

Strong authority over the lives of the less powerful was reflected in the social system that developed in the patchwork of small kingdoms and principalities of medieval Europe. The feudal system, or fief system, was the political order of government and society. Under this system, the king gave wealthy families titles of nobility and the use of land in exchange for their allegiance and promise of military service in fighting the king's enemies. The king's vassals, as they were called, promised their loyalty to the monarch.

The king's vassals, as lords of their land, promised the use of it to other men in exchange for their commitment to serve as vassals to the lord. Under the feudal system, there would be a chain of men promising allegiance to a lord, while depending on their own loyal vassals. A social hierarchy of nobility developed, with tenants-in-chief, or barons, among the highest in rank. They held lands directly from the king. But all barons and lords could make use of the territory and exact fees from their vassals for various privileges.

Feudal societies emerged only in Europe and, around the 14th century, Japan. Japanese feudalism, like that of Europe, was based on requirements of military service and conditional landownership vested with hereditary nobles. In agrarian systems outside Europe and Japan the state maintained ownership of land.

European feudalism led from conditional ownership to private ownership of property. The highest-ranking nobles, or members of the aristocracy, were able to legally own estates in their own right. Many of them worked to consolidate their holdings. And through laws of inheritance, they could pass private property on to their sons. Landownership gave the aristocracy growing wealth and political power. In time, they would seek additional rights from their monarch.

After the Norman conquest of Britain in 1066, the Norman rulers built castles to maintain control of the land and ensure that the various levels of the feudal system—peasants, knights, and barons—remained in their place and served the king. Nobles were not permitted to build castles without the king's permission. Rochester Castle in Kent, England, built in the 12th century, is one of the finest Norman castles still in existence today.

ROYAL COURTS

The feudal system came to England in the early 11th century, after William the Conqueror invaded the country. The duke of Normandy (a region of northern France), he led what became known as the Norman conquest of England. In 1066 he became its king. William subsequently granted parcels of land to his warriors and had them swear loyalty to him. In this way, he introduced the Norman feudal system and laws to England.

The king's court was the center of political life. The sovereign made major decisions affecting the territory he ruled. Issues typically involved diplomatic alliances, decisions affecting peace or war, and the appointment and dismissal of ministers. In some cases such work was delegated to others who held the favor of the king.

In theory the English king held absolute rule. But in reality he often conferred with a council of advisers before making policies or taking action. This council, called the Curia Regis, was made up of high-ranking nobles, senior church leaders, and royal advisers. The Curia Regis would eventually evolve into Parliament.

THE MAGNA CARTA

The rise of the English legislature was made possible by King John's signing of the Magna Carta. *Magna Carta* is Latin for "Great Charter" (Another word for *charter* is *constitution*).

John took the throne of England in 1199. He was an unpopular ruler whose popularity decreased when he demanded that his feudal barons pay an extra tax. They rebelled, and in 1215 civil war broke out. After confronting John on the battlefield of Runnymede, the barons forced him to sign the Magna Carta. The document guaranteed certain basic rights and other liberties for all free men in the kingdom.

By signing the document, John conceded that his power was not absolute. The Magna Carta limited the power of the king and established that he was not above the law. It also gave the king's barons the power of approval over the

During the 1300s the English Parliament was divided into two chambers. The lower chamber was the House of Commons, whose members were elected. The upper chamber was the House of Lords, whose members came from the aristocracy and inherited their positions. The right to vote for members of the House of Commons was limited to Protestant male property owners.

levying of new taxes. This would become an important power of Parliament.

The Magna Carta did not guarantee rights for all subjects. Members of the peasant class, or serfs, gained no new rights or freedoms. But the charter was the first formal document stating that the monarch, like everyone else, was bound by the rule of law. And for the first time, British law recognized the rights of individuals.

John would later say he signed the Magna Carta under duress, and he refused to honor it. But he died soon after, in 1216.

RISE OF PARLIAMENT IN ENGLAND

About 50 years after the Magna Carta, an element of democracy entered the developing parliamentary tradition. Previously, when British kings called parliaments, the members included representatives of the nobility, the clergy, and knights. But in 1264 a rebellious noble, Simon de Montfort, seized power. He summoned the usual groups to a parliamentary meeting, but also called for elected representatives from boroughs of the realm. King Henry III rejected the authority of Montfort's parliament, which met in January 1265. Montfort himself was killed in battle later in the year, and Henry regained power. But an important precedent had been set: for the first time an English parliament had included elected members.

The assembly called by King Edward I of England in 1295 became known as the "Model Parliament," because it helped create the framework by which future English legislatures would operate.

In 1295 King Edward I, wishing to raise taxes to fund his military campaigns, summoned what became known as the Model Parliament. It included commoners—ordinary people without rank or title—though peasants weren't eligible. Following the precedent set by Montfort, Edward called for Parliament to include elected citizens from boroughs and cities. The Model Parliament was a unified body, but its inclusion of nobles and commoners would pave the way for Britain's two-chamber Parliament, made up of the House of Lords and the House of Commons.

EUROPE'S REPRESENTATIVE ASSEMBLIES

Other representative assemblies and parliaments within monarchies were established in Europe during the 1200s and 1300s. They appeared in Spain, France, and Italy—and later, Germany, Scandinavia, Poland, and Hungary. In France these assemblies were called Estates-General or States-General. In some German-speaking states, the assembly was the Landtag. In Sweden, it was the Riksdag. These assemblies offered advice to the prince or king. In some cases their consent was needed for the monarch to take actions such as levying taxes.

Not everyone living in a particular state chose the members of the assembly. But the members were elected. Members of the elite classes would vote for other elites to serve as representatives in the assemblies. In theory, the nobles, clergy, and wealthy citizens serving in assemblies represented the general population of their state.

KEY IDEA

Although monarchies dominated throughout much of history, they assumed different forms from country to country, and from century to century. However, two basic forms of this system of government are absolute monarchy and constitutional monarchy. In an absolute monarchy, the king or queen holds supreme power. In a constitutional monarchy, he or she rules by consent of the people and holds limited power.

Monarchs negotiated with assemblies to get support for legal and economic policies, especially approval to raise revenue. Kings especially depended on taxes to fund wars. Power struggles often ensued. Recognizing their political leverage, members of assemblies often sought to extract concessions from the monarch. They tried to increase their own power while limiting the authority of the ruler.

PROTESTANT REFORMATION

With the end of the Middle Ages came challenges to the authority of the Roman Catholic Church. In 1517 a German monk named Martin Luther posted what would be called the Ninety-five Theses on the door of the Castle Church, in Wittenberg, Germany. The 95 statements criticized practices of the Roman Catholic Church and called for reforms. Luther would go on to question the authority of Pope Leo X, the leader of the Church. He would also come into conflict with Charles V, who ruled over the collection of mostly German-speaking states that was called the Holy Roman Empire. Luther's actions set off a period of religious and political unrest in Europe known as the Protestant Reformation.

As some monarchs chose the Protestant faith over Catholicism, religious wars broke out. One of the most devastating was the Thirty Years' War (1618–1648). That conflict between Protestants and Catholics also evolved into a struggle for power between monarchs and members of the aristocracy. Fought mostly in today's Germany, it ultimately involved most European countries.

SOVEREIGN STATES

The Thirty Years' War ended in 1648 with treaties that were part of the Peace of Westphalia. In these peace treaties the heads of major European states agreed to fixed territorial boundaries. And they required citizens to abide by laws and demands of the government rulers of those territories.

Some historians credit the Peace of Westphalia for establishing the concept of sovereign states. A sovereign state is a self-governing nation that has control over its internal affairs without interference from another power. The agreement also gave the leaders of such governments considerable power over the lives of their subjects. For example, it gave rulers the right to determine the religion of their realms.

ENGLISH CIVIL WAR AND THE GLORIOUS REVOLUTION

While the Thirty Years' War raged on the Continent, England was also undergoing great civil unrest. The conflict originated not with religion but with power. The English Civil War (1642–1651) was a conflict between the Royalists, who supported the traditional authority of the king, and the Parliamentarians, who wanted more power for Parliament. The war has also been described as a struggle between the divine right of the Crown and political rights of Parliament.

The war led to the execution of King Charles I in 1649. The victorious Parliamentary military forces declared the formation of a republican commonwealth. But after the death in 1658 of its dictatorial leader, Oliver Cromwell, the monarchy was restored.

In the late 1600s religious differences would threaten to bring on another war. By the 1680s, most British citizens were Protestants. But a Catholic monarch, King James II, sat on the throne. In 1688 members of Parliament decided James had to be replaced with a Protestant. They invited the Dutch ruler William of Orange and his wife, Mary, who was James's Protestant daughter, to invade England. Their armies entered England and James fled. With that event, which came to be known as the Glorious Revolution, Parliament assumed greater powers.

ENGLISH BILL OF RIGHTS

The following year, the legislative body passed the English Bill of Rights. This act limited the powers of the king and bolstered the authority of Parliament. The Bill of Rights established that the Crown had to seek the consent of the people, as represented in Parliament, in order to govern. The monarch could not suspend laws or levy taxes without parliamentary consent. Regular parliamentary elections had to be held, and no member

The French general Louis le Grand Condé celebrates victory over a Spanish army at Rocroi in 1643. Condé's successes on the battlefield helped bring an end to the Thirty Years' War in Europe. The peace treaties of 1648 that ended the long-running conflict established the basic principles of the modern nation-state.

of Parliament could be punished for anything he said or any position he took in the legislature. The Bill of Rights also guaranteed certain rights to all English subjects, including the right to petition the monarch without fear of retribution, and freedom from "cruel and unusual punishments." The document essentially made England a constitutional monarchy.

THE RISE OF ABSOLUTISM

While Parliament gained power in England, the Estates-General in France became weaker. The group was made up of clergy members, nobility, and wealthy citizens (known as the bourgeoisie). Beginning in the 15th century

King Louis XIV of France once outlined his philosophy of government in a simple statement: "L'état, c'est moi" ("I am the State"). This absolute monarch of the 17th and early 18th centuries was known as the Sun King because of the power he wielded in Europe.

the French kings had assumed greater centralization of lawmaking and military powers. By the 17th century France was an absolutist state.

In absolutism, the power and right to rule lies only with the monarch. Unlike medieval rulers, absolute monarchs didn't consult with nobles, councils, or other assemblies. Although they had the final word in government, absolute monarchs retained their aristocracy. Noble landowners held social privileges and some power. Western Europe also saw a growing middle class whose economic influence was significant.

Most European countries during the 1700s were ruled by absolute monarchies. They developed bureaucracies and maintained armies to enforce their authority. Absolute monarchy remained the dominant form of state in Europe until the end of the century.

COLONIALISM

At the same time, the authority of European monarchs was extended to other areas of the globe. From the 1500s on, European powers established colonies in North and South America, Africa, and Asia, eventually creating overseas empires.

The rights of individuals living under colonial rule were not considered important. Native inhabitants were not allowed to choose their system of government but were expected to submit to the authority of the mother country.

4

THE STATE OR THE INDIVIDUAL

In the late 17th and 18th centuries traditional beliefs about government were challenged. An intellectual movement known as the Enlightenment emphasized reason and the individual. Enlightenment thinkers believed that human beings were rational and capable of determining their rightful government.

SOCIAL CONTRACT AND NATURAL RIGHTS

Thomas Hobbes (1588–1679) and John Locke (1632–1704) were two 17th-century Enlightenment philosophers who questioned the notion that monarchs ruled by divine right. Hobbes, who lived during the English Civil War, was an early advocate of "social contract" theory.

Social contract theory suggests that people form society by mutual agreement—that is, by

The writings of the English philosophers Thomas Hobbes (left) and John Locke would help provide the rationale for liberal democracy.

making a contract with one another. Hobbes and later philosophers believed that monarchy originated when people consented to give up freedoms to a sovereign ruler in exchange for protection. Hobbes rejected the idea that the authority of kings comes from God. But he also didn't think a monarch should share power with a legislature. Rather, he supported the idea of absolute rule. To maintain order in society, he believed, people must submit to a sovereign with unlimited authority. And once a sovereign is installed, Hobbes said, that sovereign cannot legitimately be overthrown.

Locke, like Hobbes, rejected the divine right of kings and said that the authority of a ruler derives from the consent of the people, via the social contract. But Locke advocated limited rather than absolute governmental authority. He believed that every person has certain rights simply by virtue of being human. These rights—called natural rights—include life, liberty, and property. No government, Locke said, may justly take away these rights from its citizens without cause. In fact, governments are set up to protect people's natural rights. A government that fails to do so, Locke believed, could legitimately be overthrown.

Another philosopher who wrote about the social contract was Jean-Jacques Rousseau (1712–1778). He looked to the Athenian democracy as an ideal form of government. Rousseau supported the idea of direct democracy, in which people do not give up their rights to a sovereign ruler or delegate governing authority to elected representatives. But he recognized this form of government worked best in small communities.

DEMOCRACY VERSUS AUTOCRACY

The ideas of these and other Enlightenment philosophers would influence the thinking of British colonists living in North America. By the mid-1700s there were 13 British colonies along the Atlantic seaboard from Massachusetts to Georgia. Most had governors appointed by the British king, George III. The colonial governors appointed members of a council that held some ruling authority. And there were also elected assemblies.

The first representative legislature in the colonies had been the Virginia House of Burgesses, which first met in July 1619. Only free, white, male property owners were eligible to vote for its members. As with the colonial legislatures that developed later, the authority of the House of Burgesses was limited. All legislative acts were subject to the approval of the royal governor and the governor's council. Still, the House of Burgesses and the other colonial assemblies had the exclusive power to appropriate money—that is, the right of taxation.

British attempts to tax the colonists without the consent of their legislatures, beginning in the mid-1760s, led to escalating tensions. Colonists came to regard King George III as a tyrant. In

> "THE OBEDIENCE OF THE SUBJECT TO THE SOVEREIGN HAS ITS ROOT NOT IN CONTRACT BUT IN FORCE—THE FORCE OF THE SOVEREIGN TO PUNISH DISOBEDIENCE."
>
> —JEAN-JACQUES ROUSSEAU, *THE SOCIAL CONTRACT*

American colonists dressed as Native Americans throw crates of tea over the side of a British ship in Boston harbor, December 1773. The "Boston Tea Party," as this incident became known, was a protest against a British tax that the colonists believed to be unfair.

April 1775, fighting between royal soldiers and colonial militiamen in Massachusetts touched off the Revolutionary War.

On July 4, 1776, the 13 American colonies formally broke with Great Britain when the Continental Congress adopted the Declaration of Independence. The document, which announced the creation of the free and independent "united States of America," included many Enlightenment ideas. Especially important were principles emphasized by John Locke: that all humans have fundamental rights and that governments rule only with the consent of the people being governed. These ideas are reflected in the first lines of the Declaration:

We hold these truths to be self-evident, that all men are created equal, that they are endowed by their Creator with certain unalienable Rights, that among these are Life, Liberty and the pursuit of Happiness.—That to secure these rights, Governments are instituted among Men, deriving their just powers from the consent of the governed.

THE U.S. CONSTITUTION

The Revolutionary War finally ended in 1783. The Americans had defeated the British and secured independence.

In the first years after the war, the United States of America operated under the Articles of Confederation. This constitution set up a loose union of sovereign (self-governing) states, with a very weak central government.

In creating this sort of governmental structure, the nation's leaders hoped to prevent abuses that might arise from an overly powerful national government. They had no desire to replace the tyranny of the British monarch with home-grown tyranny.

The U.S. Constitution is a written document that embodies the fundamental principles of American government. All laws, actions by government leaders, and judicial decisions must conform to the Constitution.

But problems with the Articles of Confederation quickly emerged. Commerce suffered as the states pursued competing agendas. They maintained separate trade policies and printed their own currencies. They refused to pay off the nation's war debts. Meanwhile, the national government had almost no real authority. It didn't have the power to tax. It couldn't enforce laws, as there was no national court system. It couldn't even raise an army.

> **KEY IDEA**
>
> A federal government shares power among national and state (and local) governments.

Some American leaders recognized the need to create a stronger national government. In 1787 delegates from all of the states except Rhode Island met in Philadelphia and drafted a new constitution.

The Constitution of the United States established a federal system of government, meaning that power is shared between the national government and state (and local) governments. The Constitution also created a republic, with citizens electing officials to represent them.

To avoid creating a central government that was too powerful, America's Founding Fathers turned to the idea of separation of powers. They established three separate branches of government. The legislative branch, consisting of the two-chamber Congress, would hold the power to enact laws. The executive branch, headed by a president, would be responsible for making sure that the laws were carried out. And the judicial branch would have the power to interpret and apply the law and to judge legal disputes.

A system of checks and balances was put in place to keep one branch from exerting too much power over the others. For example, the judicial branch (federal courts) has power of judicial review. That gives the U.S. Supreme Court the power to strike down acts of Congress or state legislatures if the laws are determined to be unconstitutional. That authority was affirmed in the 1803 Supreme Court decision *Marbury v. Madison*.

The first political parties in the United States were established in the 1790s. In 1800 the nation saw the first peaceful transition of power from one political party to another, when Thomas Jefferson, of the Democratic-Republican Party, assumed the presidency. He became the country's third president, following John Adams, who belonged to the Federalist Party.

U.S. BILL OF RIGHTS

In spite of the Constitution's safeguards against the accumulation of too much power by any public official or branch of government, some people worried that the rights of individual citizens weren't explicitly protected. Nevertheless, the Constitution was ratified in 1788.

In June 1789, during the first session of Congress, James Madison of Virginia introduced a series of amendments to the Constitution. Most of the amendments were designed to guarantee the rights and freedoms of U.S. citizens. By September 1789, Congress had passed 12 amendments and sent them to the states for ratification.

Two of the amendments were rejected, but the remaining 10—known collectively as the Bill of Rights—were ratified in 1791. The Bill of Rights specifies the freedoms, protections, and legal rights of American citizens. These include the right to speak freely (including criticizing the government), freedom of assembly, freedom of religion, and the right to trial by jury.

Still, in 1791, these rights did not apply to everyone living in the United States. The more than half a million enslaved African Americans had no rights whatsoever.

THE FRENCH REVOLUTION

The American Revolution, with its ideals of liberty, equality, and individual rights, inspired rebellions against autocratic rule in other parts of the world. In France, the American example helped spark a revolution.

A mob of French citizens attacks the Bastille, July 1789. This prison-fortress in Paris was considered a symbol of the cruel way that the absolute monarchs of France had abused their power. The French Revolution resulted in major social and political changes in the country.

Under the absolute rule of French kings, the assembly known as the Estates-General wasn't convened once between 1615 and 1788. But in May 1789 King Louis XVI summoned the Estates-General in an effort to gain approval for additional taxation. The assembly consisted of representatives of three estates, or sectors of society. The First Estate (the clergy) and the Second Estate (the nobility) approved the king's request for higher taxation. But the Third Estate—the commoners—balked. Representatives of the Third Estate declared themselves the National Assembly and called for new government in France. In August 1789 the National Assembly adopted the Declaration of the Rights of Man and of the Citizen.

The influence of Enlightenment ideas and of the American Revolution—especially the Declaration of Independence—was apparent. In its preamble, the French document described the rights of man as "natural, unalienable, and sacred." Article one stated, "Men are born and remain free and equal in rights." Article two listed natural rights as "liberty, property, security, and resistance to oppression."

By 1791 the feudal privileges of the aristocracy and the clergy had been ended. In September of that year, Louis XVI was forced to accept a constitution limiting his authority. France's constitutional monarchy didn't last long, however. In September 1792 the Assembly abolished the monarchy and established France as a republic.

Much political upheaval followed. Many members of the aristocracy were put to death. So, too, were people accused of opposing the French Revolution. In 1793 both King Louis XVI and his wife, Marie-Antoinette, were beheaded.

DEMOCRACIES AND THE RIGHT TO VOTE

France's republic was short lived. In 1799 a general, Napoleon Bonaparte, seized power in a coup. Five years later, he crowned himself emperor.

But democratic ideals weren't dead in France. A republican government would be restored in 1848, overthrown in a coup three years later, and restored once again in 1870.

France was just one of a handful of European countries that emerged from the 19th century as a liberal democracy (a government that is both elected by citizens and that protects the fundamental rights and freedoms of citizens). In the

KEY IDEA

A direct democracy is very different from a democratic republic. In a direct democracy, citizens vote directly on proposed laws or other matters of government. In a democratic republic, citizens elect officials to represent their interests in government.

judgment of political scientist Francis Fukuyama, there were nine liberal democracies in Europe by 1900: Belgium, Denmark, France, Great Britain, Greece, Italy, the Netherlands, Sweden, and Switzerland. Four other liberal democracies existed elsewhere: Canada and the United States in North America, and Argentina and Chile in South America.

All of these democracies were slow to open up the political process to everyone, however. In most of the countries, the proportion of males eligible to vote was expanded through the gradual elimination of property requirements. In the United States, an additional factor was the abolishment of slavery as a result of the Civil War (1861–1865) and the ratification, in 1870, of the Fifteenth Amendment. That amendment officially gave all adult male citizens the right to vote.

But in the United States and in the world's other democracies, women continued to be second-class citizens. At the start of the 20th century, women were guaranteed the right to vote only in New Zealand, which was then a British possession.

Women would gain equal voting rights in the world's democracies at different times throughout the 20th century. In the United States, for example, that milestone came in 1920, with the ratification of the Nineteenth Amendment. Britain gave all women the right to vote in 1928, France in 1944. Swiss women didn't gain the franchise until 1971.

Russians storm government buildings in St. Petersburg, October 1917. The Russian Revolution led to the creation of the Union of Soviet Socialist Republics (USSR), the first communist state.

5

GOVERNMENT IN THE 20TH CENTURY AND BEYOND

During the 20th century, the idea of liberal democracy gained favor around the globe. By no means was this process smooth or uninterrupted. Liberal democracy advanced in fits and starts. The 20th century also witnessed the rise of new political systems that were indifferent, or even hostile, to the notion that the fundamental rights of individuals must be protected. In these systems, the needs of the state trumped all other considerations.

COMMUNISM

In 1917, in the midst of World War I, a revolution overthrew the Russian tsar (emperor), Nicholas II. After years of civil war, communists gained complete control of the country. In 1922 the Union of Soviet Socialist Republics (USSR) was officially founded. The USSR, also called the Soviet Union, was the world's first communist state.

The theoretical basis for communism came mostly from a German political philosopher, Karl Marx (1818–1883). Marx was a harsh critic of capitalism, the prevailing economic system in the advanced industrial societies of his time. Capitalism is based on competition. In a capitalist economy, individuals and companies compete for their own economic gain, and generally market forces determine the price of goods and services, as well as the wages workers receive. In the 1800s, capitalism created huge fortunes for those who owned factories and businesses. But industrial workers—men, women, and children—were paid very low wages and lived in extreme poverty. Marx believed that the working class would inevitably rise up and overthrow the class of capitalists.

There would follow a period of transition during which the state—controlled by the working class—would own all factories and businesses. Wages and the distribution of goods would still be somewhat unequal, but that situation would be temporary. After the right conditions had been created, Marx believed, human society would move to the final stage in its historical development: communism. Under communism, private property would be abolished, resources would be shared fairly among all members of society, and all distinctions of wealth and class would be eliminated. People would live in harmony. There would be no reason for government anymore, and the state itself would "wither away."

Neither the USSR nor any of the other communist governments that emerged later in the century would ever create the kind of utopian society that Marx envisioned. In fact, communist states were almost always highly repressive. And in certain cases—for example, in the USSR under Joseph Stalin (1927–1953) and China under Mao Zedong (1949–1976)—communism produced a brutal form of totalitarianism. Totalitarian regimes seek to exert control over all aspects of people's lives, private as well as public.

THE RISE AND FALL OF FASCISM

The term *totalitarianism* was popularized by the Italian dictator Benito Mussolini. In the 1920s, Mussolini seized power and championed a new kind of government, known as fascism. Fascism denied that citizens had any rights the state was obligated to respect. Rather, citizens were expected to serve the state and blindly obey their leaders. "The Fascist conception of life," Mussolini wrote, "stresses the importance of the State and accepts the individual only in so far as his interests coincide with those of the State."

Fascism appealed to an extreme sense of nationalism. It promoted an aggressive foreign policy and glorified violence.

Mussolini and his fascist ideas inspired other would-be dictators around the world. The most infamous was Germany's Adolf Hitler. In the early 1920s Hitler became leader of a small political party, the National Socialist German Workers' Party, better known as the Nazi Party. By 1933 he had exploited political gridlock, economic distress, and social unrest to have himself named head of Germany's democratic government. Once in power, Hitler quickly eliminated democracy in Germany and established a brutal totalitarian regime, which he headed.

In the years after World War I, dictators like Adolf Hitler of Germany and Benito Mussolini of Italy used discontent among the people of their countries, as well as violence and intimidation, to gain power.

Nazi Germany's aggression against its neighbors eventually touched off World War II, the bloodiest conflict in history. The war began in September 1939, with Germany's invasion of Poland. Germany would be joined by Italy and Japan in a military alliance known as the Axis. The Axis Powers were finally defeated in 1945. Fascism was completely discredited as a governing philosophy. But the war had claimed an estimated 60 million lives.

THE COLD WAR

The Soviet Union and the United States, allies in the fight against Nazi Germany, emerged after World War II as adversaries. The two countries represented opposing political systems. The United States championed liberal democracy (including capitalist economics); the Soviet Union promoted communism.

Between the late 1940s and the late 1980s, the two superpowers engaged in a struggle for global political dominance. That struggle was known as the cold war. While the United States and the Soviet Union didn't fight each other directly during the cold war, they did support opposing sides in numerous national and regional conflicts. They also propped up governments and supported leaders perceived as friendly to their cause.

The Soviet Union established a bloc of communist states in Eastern Europe. When people in these satellite states showed an inclination to reject or temper communism—for example, in Hungary in 1956 and Czechoslovakia in 1968—Soviet leaders responded with crushing military force.

For its part, the United States—despite a professed commitment to liberal democracy—supported various right-wing dictatorships during the cold war. And in a several instances (Iran, 1953; Guatemala, 1954; Chile, 1972), the United States even sponsored or provided aid to coups that overthrew democratically elected but left-leaning leaders. Opposition to communism and the containment of Soviet expansion trumped other considerations.

During the 1950s, 1960s, and 1970s the United States sent soldiers to fight in Korea (top) and Vietnam (left inset) in an attempt to prevent the spread of communist governments in Asia.

END OF COLONIALISM

If the cold war dominated international affairs, another major trend played out concurrently: decolonization. In the decades after World War II—particularly between the 1950s and 1970s—European countries relinquished their overseas colonies. Dozens of new, independent states emerged.

Most former colonies pursued a democratic form of government upon achieving independence. In some cases, democracy took firm root. India is a prime example. British rule over India ended in 1947, and by 1952 a multiparty democracy with universal suffrage had been established. India was, and continues to be, the world's most populous democracy.

Often, however, the democracies of newly independent countries did not endure. In Africa, almost every former colony would lapse into some form of dictatorship.

One of the most well known of Africa's oppressive governments was that of South Africa. It was by no means typical, however. South Africa didn't gain independence in the postwar wave of decolonization. It had gained practical, if not official, independence in 1910. In 1948 South Africa's whites-only government established a system of racial segregation known as apartheid. Under apartheid, the black majority was denied all political rights. Apartheid continued even after South Africa officially became a republic in 1961. It was finally overturned in 1991, and elections open to all South Africans were first held three years later.

RIGHTS FOR ALL

Even in a democracy the minority can be oppressed. This was the case for blacks in the United States during the first half of the 20th century. In theory, African Americans were guaranteed equal rights under the U.S. Constitution with the ratification of the Thirteenth Amendment (1865), which abolished slavery; the Fourteenth Amendment (1868), which gave anyone born or naturalized in the United States, including former slaves, full citizenship and required equal protection under the law; and the Fifteenth Amendment (1870), which gave blacks equal voting rights. In

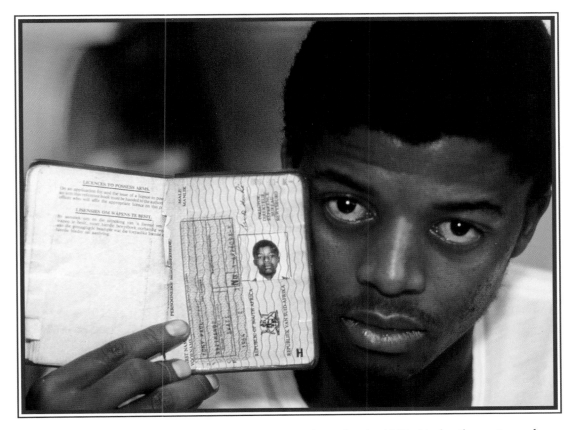

A black South African shows his government-issued passbook, 1985. Under the system of racial segregation known as apartheid—which was in effect in South Africa from 1948 until 1991—nonwhites (blacks, Asians, and people of mixed race, known as Coloureds) were required to carry a passbook at all times. This provided a means by which the government could monitor them and limit their movement.

reality, African Americans were prevented from exercising their full rights as citizens, especially in the South, for a century after the end of slavery.

In southern states, blacks were prevented from voting through poll taxes and literacy tests. Jim Crow laws required racial segregation in public places. African Americans in the South were second-class citizens, enjoying neither the political rights nor the social freedom of whites.

The passage of the Civil Rights Act of 1964 outlawed discrimination based on an individual's race, color, religion, sex, or national origin.

Legislators and African-American civil rights leaders watch as President Lyndon B. Johnson signs the 1965 Voting Rights Act. The act ensured that black Americans would have the same opportunity to vote for their political leaders that white citizens enjoyed.

Segregation in businesses and public facilities was forbidden. In this way, the U.S. government guaranteed rights of personal liberty.

To guarantee the rights of African Americans to participate in elections, Congress passed the Twenty-fourth Amendment, which banned poll taxes, and passed the Voting Rights Act in 1965. It called for federal workers to register black voters. And it prohibited the use of literacy tests as a condition for voting. It took many years for the U.S. government to recognize the need to protect an oppressed minority. But eventually legal protections were put in place to support the basic rights of all citizens.

A DEMOCRATIC FUTURE?

In the late 1980s, the Soviet Union ceased propping up the regimes of Eastern Europe. One by one, these communist governments fell. The Soviet Union itself collapsed in 1991.

The end of the cold war was followed by a rise in the number of democracies around the world. Most of the formerly communist countries of Eastern Europe became democratic. Latin America and East Asia also witnessed an upsurge in democratic governments during the 1990s.

At that time, some political scientists asserted confidently that the trend toward liberal democracy was irreversible. By the first decade of the 21st century, however, such confidence appeared premature, if not entirely misplaced. Various governments that had appeared to be on a path to democratization—including Russia, Venezuela, Nigeria, and Thailand—took a turn toward authoritarianism.

Still, democracy may prevail in the long run. The idea that a legitimate government must have the consent of the governed took centuries to develop. But that idea has taken root, inspiring people all over the globe to demand freedom and respect for fundamental human rights.

CHAPTER NOTES

p. 8: "to direct the thinking . . ." quoted in "The Berlin Wall," *Newseum*, http://www.newseum.org/berlinwall/two_sides_one_story/a_clash_of_ideas/newspapers.htm

p. 8: "[A] state is a . . ." Max Weber, "Politics as a Vocation," in A. P. Thakur, *Weber's Political Sociology* (New Delhi, India: Global Vision Publishing House, 2006), p. 44.

p. 17: "War made the state . . ." Charles Tilly, ed., *The Formation of National States in Western Europe* (Princeton, N.J.: Princeton University Press, 1975), p. 42.

p. 17: "Life, liberty and property . . ." Frédéric Bastiat, quoted in David Gordon, *Secession, State, and Liberty* (New Brunswick, N.J.: Transaction Publishers, 2009), p. 39.

p. 38: "The obedience of the . . ." John Morley, *Rousseau, Volume 2* (London: Chapman and Hall, 1873), p. 180.

p. 40: "We hold these truths . . ." "Declaration of Independence," *National Archives: The Charters of Freedom.* http://www.archives.gov/exhibits/charters/declaration_transcript.html

p. 44: "natural, unalienable, and sacred," "Declaration of the Rights of Man—1789," Yale Law School: *The Avalon Project.* http://avalon.law.yale.edu/18th_century/rightsof.asp

p. 44: "Men are born . . ." Ibid.

p. 44: "liberty, property, security, . . ." Ibid.

p. 49: "The Fascist conception . . ." Benito Mussolini, quoted in Jeffrey Thompson Schnapp, ed., *A Primer of Italian Fascism* (Lincoln: University of Nebraska Press, 2000), p. 48.

CHRONOLOGY

CA. 8000 BC: Invention of agriculture leads nomadic tribal societies to establish small settlements, which can be defined as states.

CA. 4000 BC: Large cities are established in Egypt, Mesopotamia, China, and India; social hierarchies develop in bureaucratic governments headed by monarchs.

CA. 2100–2050 BC: Appearance of first written laws produced by the Sumerian civilization.

CA. 1750 BC: The Babylonian king makes public a system of rules known as Hammurabi's code of law.

FIFTH CENTURY BC: Democracy in the Greek city-state of Athens reaches its height.

AD 534: Roman laws are collected and systemized under the rule of the Byzantine emperor Justinian.

1066: William of Normandy defeats the Anglo-Saxons in England. As the English king he will introduce the feudal system.

1215: The power of the monarch is limited in England when rebellious barons force King John to sign the Magna Carta.

1265: In England the first elected Parliament meets.

1517: Martin Luther posts the Ninety-five Theses at Wittenberg, which sparks the Protestant Reformation—a period of great religious and political unrest in Europe.

1648: The Peace of Westphalia ends war between Protestants and Catholics and gives rise to sovereign states.

1689: The British Parliament passes the Bill of Rights, which greatly reduces the power of the king; Parliament establishes a constitutional monarchy in England.

1776: With the signing of the Declaration of Independence, the British colonies in North America assert independence from Britain and form a government based on the rights of individuals.

1789: The French Revolution begins. France's National Assembly adopts the Declaration of the Rights of Man and of the Citizen.

1791:   The U.S. Bill of Rights, which guarantees rights and freedoms to citizens, is ratified.

1832:   The British Parliament passes the first in a series of Reform Acts that increase suffrage for male voters in England.

1870:   The Fifteenth Amendment to the U.S. Constitution prohibits denying voting rights based on race, color, or former status as a slave.

1893:   New Zealand becomes the first nation to grant women the right to vote.

1920:   The Nineteenth Amendment to the U.S. Constitution, which gives women the right to vote, is ratified.

1945:   The end of World War II is followed by a rise in the number of democracies in the world; an international organization of countries, the United Nations (UN), is established.

1948:   The UN Universal Declaration of Human Rights calls for governments to abide by the will of the people.

1964:   In the United States, the Civil Rights Act guarantees rights and freedoms for African Americans.

1989–91:   The collapse of communism in Eastern Europe and the Soviet Union is followed by the establishment of democratic republics.

GLOSSARY

ABSOLUTE MONARCHY—a form of government in which the monarch holds power that is not limited by laws or a government constitution.

AUTOCRATIC—describing a ruler or state with absolute power.

BUREAUCRAT—an official in a government department.

CAPITALISM—an economic system that permits the ownership of private property, allows individuals and companies to compete for their own economic gain, and generally lets free market forces determine the price of goods and services.

CONFEDERATION—a political union created by treaty or constitution.

COMMUNISM—a political and economic system that champions the elimination of private property and common ownership of goods, for the benefit of all members of society.

CONSTITUTION—a document that contains the system of fundamental laws and principles that determines the nature, functions, and limits of a government.

DEMOCRATIC REPUBLIC—a system of government in which political power is retained by the people, who choose representatives through elections.

MONARCHY—a form of government headed by a king, queen, or emperor.

OLIGARCHY—a form of government in which a small group of people holds power, often for their own benefit.

PARLIAMENT—a legislative assembly or lawmaking body.

PARLIAMENTARY DEMOCRACY—a political system in which parliament selects the government (the executive branch, consisting of prime minister and cabinet ministers) based on political party strength as expressed in public elections.

REPUBLIC—a representative democracy in which representatives elected by the people (and not the people themselves) vote on legislation.

SOVEREIGN—possessing supreme power.

TYRANNY—absolute rule by a single person; dictatorship.

FURTHER READING

FOR OLDER READERS

Fukuyama, Francis. *The Origins of Political Order: From Prehuman Times to the French Revolution*. New York: Farrar, Straus, and Giroux, 2011.

Glendon, Mary Ann. *The Forum and the Tower; How Scholars and Politicians Have Imagined the World, from Plato to Eleanor Roosevelt*. New York: Oxford University Press, 2011.

FOR YOUNGER READERS

Cox, Alexander, et al., eds. *Who's in Charge?* New York: DK Publishing, 2010.

Friedman, Mark. *The Democratic Process*. New York: Children's Press, 2012.

Robinson, Mary. *Every Human Has Rights: A Photographic Declaration for Kids*. Washington, D.C.: National Geographic, 2009.

INTERNET RESOURCES

http://avalon.law.yale.edu/subject_menus/18th.asp

> The Avalon Project of Yale Law School provides the texts of important documents in history. Included on the "18th Century Documents" page are links to the Declaration of Independence and the Declaration of the Rights of Man and the Citizen.

http://www.ourdocuments.gov/content.php?page=milestone

> This site, compiled by the National Archives and Records Administration, features links to "100 Milestone Documents" in the history of the United States, from 1776 to 1965. It features background information and transcripts of documents.

http://www.state.gov/r/pa/ei/bgn/index.htm

> "Background Notes" provides up-to-date information from the U.S. Department of State on countries around the world. Included are facts about their people, history, government, economy, and foreign relations.

Publisher's Note: The Web sites listed on these pages were active at the time of publication. The publisher is not responsible for Web sites that have changed their address or discontinued operation since the date of publication.

INDEX

Numbers in **bold italics** refer to captions.

CONTRIBUTORS

Senior Consulting Editor **Timothy J. Colton** is Morris and Anna Feldberg Professor of Government and Russian Studies and is the chair of the Department of Government at Harvard University. His books include *The Dilemma of Reform in the Soviet Union* (1986); *Moscow: Governing the Socialist Metropolis* (1995), which was named best scholarly book in government and political science by the Association of American Publishers; *Transitional Citizens: Voters and What Influences Them in the New Russia* (2000); and *Popular Choice and Managed Democracy: The Russian Elections of 1999 and 2000* (with Michael McFaul, 2003). Dr. Colton is a member of the editorial board of World Politics and Post-Soviet Affairs.

LeeAnne Gelletly is the author of several books for young adults, including biographies of Harriet Beecher Stowe, Mae Jemison, Roald Dahl, Ida Tarbell, and John Marshall.